Here's what people are saying about *How Kids Make Friends:*

"Lonnie Michelle has written what could be your child's first self-help book - *How Kids Make Friends...Secrets for making lots of friends, no matter how shy you are.* It definitely, yet gently, shows kids in their own language that acquiring friendships is a matter of the choices you make and the responsibility you take for the task - not something beyond their reach. This is a valuable lesson, which if generalized can extend to many other life skills as well. I highly recommend it."
> --Michael S. Broder, Ph.D., author of *The Art of Living Single* (Avon Books)

"I LOVED this book! By the time my mom and I were finished reading it, my face hurt from smiling so much."
> -- Julie R, age 9

"Lonnie Michelle's book comes at a good time for an audience of parents, teachers, therapists and others who enjoy helping children grow and make their way in this complex society...It is written in a relaxed and upbeat manner with lots of specific suggestions and strategies that children can adopt for meeting new people, learning what to say, and what to do. Ms. Michelle doesn't just give advice: she has many explanations for why she suggests youngsters do as she says..."
> -- Rita P. Sussman, Ph.D. Clinical Psychologist

"*How Kids Make Friends* is a simple yet practical step-by-step blueprint written for any child for making friends."
> -- New York Times best-selling author Jack Canfield, *Chicken Soup for the Kid's Soul*

"Lonnie Michelle takes a sensitive subject and makes it a comfortable one; for both parent and child. With a new house, new neighborhood and new school ahead of us, this was just the book our family needed to jump that social hurdle and make new friends." --Lisa Roberts, author of *How to Raise a Family and A Career Under One Roof.*

"...a gem of a book, both for children and parents. Each page offers the child a new tip and new possibilities. With each new strategy comes greater confidence and opening up to rewarding experiences. This book should be required reading for all elementary and middle school-aged childfen." -- Gerald D. Oster, Ph.D., Clinical Associate Professor of Psychiatry, University of Maryland Medical School. Co-author, *Helping Your Depressed Teenager: A guide for parents and caregivers* (Wiley, 1995)

"*How Kids Make Friends* is highly recommended for children ages six and up, parents, grandparents, educators and libraries."
> -- The Midwest Book Review

"WOW yourself by effortlessly raising your self esteem *now*. Read this book."
> -- New York Times best-selling author Mark Victor Hansen, *Chicken Soup for The Soul*

How Kids Make Friends

...Secrets for making lots
of friends, no matter
how shy you are

Lonnie Michelle

Freedom Publishing Co.
2530 Crawford Avenue
Evanston, IL 60201
www.freedompub.com

ACKNOWLEDGMENTS
Our pre-teen kids were moving to a new neighborhood for the first time in their lives, and they were concerned about making friends at their new school. Although our family hadn't moved in over ten years, my husband and I had moved a combined nine times by the time we were in high school. While speaking to one of our children about making new friends, we realized that there are no classes in school that teach one of the most important social skills every child (and adult) should have – how to make friends.

With our sincere desire to help our children make their transition as easy as possible, and by combining our experience with substantial research, we have been led to write this practical and enjoyable book on making friends. Our kids have consulted on this book from the beginning to make sure that kids their own age will enjoy reading it, and will respond to the easy and entertaining ways we present its message. We thank them very much for their help.

International Standard Book Number: 0-9638152-1-0
Library of Congress Catalog Card Number: 95-60589
Printed in the United States of America

Cover design and illustration by Lightbourne Images copyright © 2000
Illustrations by Teresa McHugh

How Kids Make Friends is available at special discounts on bulk purchases for sales promotions, premiums, fundraising or educational use. For details, please contact the Special Sales Department at Freedom Publishing Company.

Table of Contents

Foreword to Parents

Kids who are skilled at making friends have many advantages over most other children. The ability to make friends helps a child build a healthy self-esteem at a very early age. Children who make friends easily tend to be happier and feel better about themselves. If your child is fortunate enough to learn these skills when he is young, there is a strong likelihood that he or she will grow up to be a leader, and have a healthy self-esteem throughout life.

The ideas in this book present an early training ground for a framework of success habits which will lead to greater achievement as time goes on. Learning these habits at an early age is one of the best things that could happen to your child. We encourage you and your child to read this book enthusiastically!

The following is a practical, easy guide of simple principles every child can use to learn how to make as many of the kinds of friends as he wants as he goes through life. By choosing their own friends, kids are happier and are less likely to end up with groups who may not be the best influence on them.

This book is for your child. Although your input is important, it is critical for children to read this book as well, and learn these principles for themselves. They will achieve greater self-esteem if they are able to grasp these concepts on their own.

Even though you understand that making friends is important, you must also realize that kids can never have too many friends. If a child with a small circle of friends loses one because the friend's family moves away, or because the two have a falling out, that child may be crushed. However, if the child has many friends, their companionship will make the loss easier to deal with.

Chapter 9 will show the important part you can play in helping your child successfully make and keep friends. Although you cannot outwardly tell your children whom to choose as their friends, by being a part of the friendship process, you strongly influence the circle of friends they select.

Children won't make friends by staying cooped up in their room. Encourage your child to join after school activities, visit a schoolmate after school or on the weekend, or invite someone to the house. Good communication between you and your child will tell you how well he is getting along with his playmates.

It is important always to remember to treat your child with respect when he has a friend over. When you treat your child as a person who deserves respect, you set the example for his friend to do the same.

Show this book to your child's teacher. The teacher may choose to reinforce the ideas in this book by encouraging role-playing in class, thus giving your child some great practice, and developing confidence while having fun with classmates.

Chapter 1

BEGINNINGS

It's not easy to make friends, is it? Don't be embarrassed if you feel that way, because making friends is hard for many people. One of the most popular books ever written, How to Win Friends and Influence People by Dale Carnegie, sold over FIFTEEN MILLION copies. That book is for **adults** who need help making friends. Just think - if it's that hard for adults to make friends, it must be hard for kids as well.

Making friends is one of the most important things you can do in your life. Good friends will be there when you need them, to have fun with, play with, do homework with, share with, and just to talk to. Even though making friends is **so** important, there are no classes in school on how to make friends. Do you think that learning how to make friends is as important and useful a subject as science and history? I do!

When you're bored and you have nothing to do, do you sometimes feel sorry for yourself because you don't have a friend to play with? That happens to everyone at one time or another. Instead of being upset, you can decide to make lots of friends so you don't have time to be unhappy. You will learn here how to make all the friends that you want. You just have to make the effort!

Making friends is more than just meeting people. During your lifetime, you will meet hundreds, maybe thousands of people. But some of the people that you meet will be really nice and you will want them for your friends. This book will show you easy ways to make friends with those people. Even though, right now, you think that will be hard to do, just wait until you have finished reading this book. You will get some great ideas about meeting people and making all the friends you want. It's easier than you think - and it's fun!

Chapter 2

WHY IS MAKING FRIENDS SO IMPORTANT?

Sometimes kids who don't have good friends get upset with themselves and don't feel important. You may feel you are a failure if everyone else seems to have friends and you don't. When you look around the school and see other kids playing together while you're all alone, you may feel there is something wrong with you. Did you ever think that maybe the only thing wrong is that you haven't *tried* to be friends with anyone? Maybe you're shy or don't feel that you deserve to be someone's friend. Just because someone else has lots of friends doesn't mean that you can't be their friend too.

Why are some kids more popular than others? You'll notice that they aren't always the biggest, the strongest, the best athletes, or the best looking. Often they are the ones who are more talkative; the ones who aren't afraid to go up to someone and start talking to them about different things. That's how lots of kids make friends and become popular. They know what to say and when to say it. We'll give you plenty of examples of what you can say and do to make all the friends you want!

Chapter 3

LIKE YOURSELF FIRST

You must feel good about yourself before you can expect someone else to want to be your friend. How can you expect someone else to like you, if you don't like yourself? Can you believe that some kids feel that they don't deserve to have any good friends? Are you one of those kids?

If so, take the time to make a list. The list will include all of the things you are good at. Start with school. Are you good at math, spelling, science, history or reading? Are you good at a foreign language? Is your handwriting neat? Do you try hard to get good grades? Are you liked by some of the kids in your class, or your teacher? Don't forget - write down all of the good things.

Now what about outside of school? Are you good at any sports? How about running, football, baseball or basketball, golf or volleyball? Can you roller skate, ice skate or ride your bike well? If so, write it all down.

Do people think of you as a nice person? Are you liked at school, in your neighborhood, by those who know you? Are you helpful around the house? Do you keep your room clean, or help out at family parties? Do you take the time to help your family when they need it?

Once you write down all of your good points, you will see that you are indeed a special person - you *do* deserve to have friends, just like everyone else!

Always try to have a good attitude toward people. Someone who has a bad attitude all the time isn't very pleasant to be with. People won't want to spend a lot of time with that person. I know I wouldn't!

You should always try to do the right thing. If you call kids names, start fights, or somehow hurt others, you won't feel good about yourself because you know that you are doing something that is wrong. But if you don't do these things, others will like and respect you. They'll know you are friendly and not mean. Everyone wants to spend more time with friendly kids than with nasty ones.

Personal hygiene is especially important. If someone smells bad, you may not want to spend lots of time with them. Make sure that your breath is fresh (by brushing your teeth carefully every morning), and that you don't smell bad (by wearing clean clothes each day, bathing or showering, and using deodorant).

You should **treat other kids as you want them to treat you**. If you remember this, it will be easier for you to keep the friends you want. When you are nice to others, they will be nice to you. But if you are mean or nasty to them, don't share with them, or treat them badly, they will treat you the same way. You are better off being nice to them, so they will be nice in return! In other words, however you want someone to act toward you is how you should act toward them.

Say something nice to three people a day! This is a habit that you should practice every day, starting today. It isn't hard to compliment three people a day, if you know what to look for.

Let's say you go up to someone you recognize and notice her book bag. Is it new? Ask her where she got it. Notice her clothing. Find out where you can get a pair of shoes like the ones she is wearing. Did someone you know get a new pair of glasses or braces? You can tell them that they look good with the new addition. If you do this, I *promise* that great things will happen to you. In fact, you may even receive compliments of your own. By looking for good things about other people, you develop a positive attitude. Everyone likes a person who makes a habit of complimenting others. After that, you will find it easy to start talking to kids when you can find something you know they will want to talk about.

What kid doesn't want to talk about himself or herself? That's every kid's favorite topic! We'll talk more about this later in Chapter 6 because it's so important. But don't forget - if you take the time to talk about the person you are with instead of yourself, you will automatically make friends!

Chapter 4

WHO SHOULD BE YOUR FRIEND?

Figure out who you want to be your friends. You will probably want someone who is a lot like you with many of the same interests. You will want someone who smiles a lot. If you are quiet, you may like someone who is quiet like you, or you may prefer someone who is more talkative. If you are loud and like to run around, you will want someone who runs around like you do. If you like to play the piano and play on your computer, you may not get along well with someone who would rather play outdoor sports and doesn't like the computer or piano.

You will have different kinds of friends during your life. Some will be kids at school or in your neighborhood that you talk to sometimes but don't spend a lot of time with. Other kids will be closer friends. These are the friends you play with more often, and have a good time with. Then there are your best friends. Best friends don't happen right away. You develop best friends by spending lots of time with them, and sharing many experiences together over a long period of time.

You will find that you want to be friends with someone you feel comfortable with. And you will feel comfortable with someone who has the same interests you have.

Chapter 5

HOW DO YOU MEET PEOPLE?

One of the simplest ways to meet people is also one of the easiest. **Smile.** If you go up to someone and you are smiling, you may not have to say a word. Since most people don't smile, the other person may start talking to you just to ask, "Why are you smiling?" Then you can answer them, "Because today has been a great day," or "I'm looking forward to my next class," or "I thought that would be the best way to introduce myself to you." See how easy it is? When you smile, kids think you are friendly. When you scowl, people think you are upset or mean.

You can practice smiling at yourself in the mirror. Notice the difference in your eyes when you smile. Can you see that your eyes look more friendly looking when you smile and more serious when you frown? Most people look at your eyes when you meet, and your smile will give your eyes a "friendly" look.

Which of these people would

you rather be friends with?

Once you have practiced your smile in the mirror until you feel comfortable, practice smiling at your family. When you feel comfortable doing that, you can start smiling at different kids at school.

Get involved in different activities after school; dance, sports, music, piano, scouts, art classes, etc.

Sit with different people at lunch so you can meet them. Sometimes you won't find your friends to sit with, so take a chance and sit with other kids. If you look at them and pay attention to what they have to say, you may be able to join in their conversation, and start to make some new friends.

Talk to different kids in your class about homework. This is easy to do because everyone has to get their homework done, and it is easy to think of questions to ask them. It is also easy to ask if they want to do the homework together. This makes homework more fun, and it's usually easier to get it done with someone's help.

    Invite kids who are alone to join your group for lunch, studying, playing at recess, etc. The person you invite will like you right away. This increases your number of friends.

When you meet someone, say that person's name in your mind five times, so you won't forget it. People's names are very important to them, and when you remember their name, it makes them feel very special. Whenever you make someone else feel special, they will like you right away.

Remember what we said about saying something nice to three people a day? If you do that every day to different people, soon you will have more friends than you know what to do with!

Chapter 6

HOW DO YOU BECOME THEIR FRIEND?

Now that you've met someone, how do you become their friend? There are many easy ways. The easiest way is to **make them feel important**. When someone is talking about you, or asking questions about you, don't you feel important? Kids who have lots of friends show an interest in those friends. So when you first start talking to someone, ask them about themselves, and pay attention to what they have to say! Good questions to ask are "Who is your teacher?" or "What is your favorite class?" or "Where do you live?"

Remember, if you talk about the *other* person they will know that you are interested in them, and they will begin to like you. Once they like you, they will want to know more about *you*, and will start asking you questions about yourself. Why? Because the thing that people like to talk about the most is *themselves!*

Learn how to talk to people. It is important to look into their eyes. When you do that, they know that you are paying attention to what they have to say. If that's not easy for you to do, practice first with your family. It is important that you make others feel important by listening to them and talking about them. Don't forget, people like to talk about themselves the most. If you talk about them, you will get their attention, and they will want to talk to you much more!

Once you have shown someone that you have an interest in them, and that you are likeable (by asking them questions about themselves), you can ask them over to your house after school. Why? To do homework if you're in the same class, to play if you don't have any homework, or just to "hang out". But don't ask someone to just "hang out" until you are close friends. Kids who aren't close friends yet don't want to be bored, and will want to do something that's fun. Make sure you have something that's fun to do if you invite them to your house.

Why should you invite someone over to your house to play? If you are too shy to talk to someone at school, the easiest way to be friendly is to invite them to your house after school. This is a good idea for many reasons. First of all, when you invite a new friend to your house, you are letting him know that you want to be friendly with him without actually saying so. Also, you will have a chance to play with him without any of his friends joining in and spoiling your fun. This way, you can show your new friend that you are fun to be with, too.

When a new friend comes to your house, you must have some good ideas of things the two of you can do. Make sure that you plan different things to do ahead of time with your mom or dad. You don't want your friend to be bored at your house. When you ask someone over, find out what he likes to do, so you can plan ahead. If he likes to play baseball, make sure he brings his baseball glove over, and that you have a ball and bat handy. If he likes to play other games, make sure that you are prepared.

See if your mom can have cookies or other food in the house so you can have a snack. This never fails. Everyone loves snack time!

Chapter 7

HOW DO YOU GET CLOSE FRIENDS?

Soon you will have lots of friends. How do you know which of your friends will be your closest? These will be the ones who you have the most fun with. They will be the ones who you feel most comfortable with and who like many of the same things that you like.

You will be able to trust them and tell them just about anything, including your secrets. And they will like to just hang out with you as much as you like to hang out with them. The kids you enjoy being with, without doing anything special, are the kids who will be your closest friends.

A close friend is also someone you laugh a lot with, even if something isn't really funny. But the best thing about a close friend is that, even if you have disagreements, you will feel comfortable making up with him, and can depend on him to be your friend the next day.

Chapter 8

THINGS YOU CAN DO TOGETHER

When you start making friends, you want to find a variety of different things to do so no one gets bored. Don't be the kind of kid who says, "I don't know. What do you want to do?" If you always have some good ideas about what to do, your friends will enjoy spending more time with you. You can add to the following list:

* Start a hobby together, like collecting baseball cards, stamps, pennies...

* Start a class together, like dance class, piano, acting, arts and crafts, gymnastics, etc. You could even pretend to have your own class. Write a small play together and perform it in front of the family or some of your neighbors.

* Have a snack together. Make your own sundaes, cookies, milk shakes.

* Write to a pen pal. You can even write letters to each other. Several children's magazines offer pen pal connections. Go to the library with your friend and check it out.

* Cook something (with the help of Mom or Dad) like cookies, cake, cupcakes, or brownies. Did you ever try to make a pizza?

* Do you have any board games that you can play? There are also many card games that are fun and easy to learn. Ask your mom or dad to teach you some of them.

* Play on a computer, if you have one. You can go to the library and borrow software that contains hundreds of games and programs.

* Play sports in your back yard, or go to a nearby park. You can play catch, frisbee, hockey, or dozens of different games outside. How many games can *you* think of?

Page 47

*   Play music, or try out some of the latest dance steps from your favorite music videos or TV shows.

*   Try arts and crafts. Painting is always fun. How about fingerpainting? It could be fun to collect twigs and leaves outside and make a collage.

* What about making up poems and writing them down?

* Put together a large puzzle.

* Play school. If you don't have a chalkboard, you could even use chalk on the sidewalk (don't worry - the rain will wash it away!).

* Learn magic tricks and practice them on each other. Magic is a great way to meet kids at school. If you learn a good trick, and show it to people during lunch break or recess, you will be able to get their attention easily.

* Find other outside activities like jumprope, roller skating, roller blading, flying a kite, bike riding, swimming, hopscotch, frisbee, etc.

* Find other inside activities like card games, bingo, charades, crossword puzzles, hangman, tic-tac-toe, etc.

ADD YOUR IDEAS FOR ACTIVITIES HERE. THIS CAN BE A PERMANENT REFERENCE LIST FOR YOU.

*

*

*

*

*

*

*

*

*

*

*

*

*

*

With this list, you'll never be bored!

Chapter 9

GETTING HELP FROM YOUR PARENTS

Kids! Ask your parents to read this chapter. They can really help you make friends if they do the things we discuss below.

Mom and Dad, here are some things that you should do to help your child not only make friends easier, but also gain confidence and self-esteem. Clearly, the more friends your child has, the more self-esteem and confidence he or she will have. Likewise, the more assurance your child has, the easier it will be for him to approach kids and make new friends. Please pay attention to the following:

*   Encourage your kids to make more friends by having them invite someone new to your house at least once each month.

Which household will your friend come back to?

*   Treat your child and his guest with respect. A
      mean parent (or one who doesn't seem friendly)
      may scare a potential new friend away from your
      child.

*   Offer your child's friend a snack (milk and cookies,
      etc.). If the guest feels welcome in your home, he
      will feel comfortable enough to return again and a-
      gain.

*   Make sure that you and your child have prepared
      for the guest, and that there is plenty to do, so no
      one gets bored.

*   Be a friend to your child. It's important to be a par-
      ent, and to teach him right from wrong, but also be
      a friend.

*   Don't scold or ridicule your child in front of his
      friends.

*   Occasionally invite your child's best friend on a short trip with the family (camping, skiing, lunch, bowling, a movie, etc.).

*   When appropriate, take pictures of your child with his friends, and make an album with those pictures so he can see them when he gets older. Remember to put the year and name of the friend on the back of the picture.

*   Help your child with his homework when he needs it. Take an interest. If you don't, he won't either. By your taking an interest, you are showing him the importance of getting good grades without preaching. The better the grades your child gets, the better the chance that he will associate with others who are achieving good grades as well.

*   Encourage your child to earn some spending money doing chores around the house or the neighborhood (mowing lawns, raking leaves, shovelling snow, cleaning windows or yards, etc.).

This way, he'll have some money to spend with his playmates. Having his own money gives him self-esteem.

* Pay attention to what your child has to say.

* When your kids have friends over, respect their privacy.

* Always encourage your child to improve him or herself.

* Set good examples. If you reject bad habits (smoking, drinking, drugs, etc.), there is an excellent chance that your child will, also.

* Encourage outside activities (dance, sports, scouts, etc.) where your child can meet kids outside of school.

* Make sure your kids finish their homework before they spend time with their friends.

*   Set aside some one on one time with each of your children each week. This is a great time for you to get closer and bond.

*   Show an interest in your youngster's life, including friendships, school, health, etc. Don't be afraid to ask questions during the time you spend together.

*   Don't ever lie to your kids - your credibility is critical to them. One lie, and they will question what you have to say in the future.

*   Don't be a "yes" parent. Children need discipline, and the word "no" is the best word in the English language for discipline.

*   Make a point to laugh together every day. Making the effort to find something funny will make you more pleasant to be around and spend time with. This also teaches your child to use humor in his relationships with friends.

*   Encourage your kids to make friends by complimenting them on their choices. They won't find too many "perfect" friends, so don't force them to set unrealistic goals.

*   Help them get together with their new friends by arranging transportation to and from each other's homes and for any planned activities away from home.

*   Find alternatives to watching television; show them some creativity.

*   Develop an image in your child's friends' minds of being cheerful, helpful and friendly, not mean, demanding or intimidating. This could strain or ruin a friendship with one of your children's playmates.

*   Get to know each other better by telling stories.

*   Encourage your children to take risks, by approaching other children and beginning a conversation.

*   Be aware of your body language. Kids can sense your feelings, even though you may not verbalize them.

*   As important as friendships are, don't let your kids forget Family!

*   Never stop telling your child that you love him, and he will never stop telling you. However, don't do it in front of his friends.

*   Read this book with your child at least once a year. This reinforces your kid's skills and knowledge, and reminds you of what you may have forgotten during the year. With practice, these skills will become lifetime habits.

Chapter 10

SUMMARY

Here is a SUMMARY of what you have learned. If you remember these golden rules, you will never have trouble making friends.

1) Show people that you are interested in them. This is much easier than trying to get them interested in you. Ask them a question about themselves, and be a good listener while they happily answer you. When you show interest in your friends, you make them feel important. Everyone likes to feel important. By using this approach, people will flock to you.

2) Smile. Not only will the smile convince those around you that you are happy, but it is very hard for you to be upset about something if you are smiling. People like to be around happy people.

3) Remember people's names. Just as important as showing people that you are interested in them, is knowing their name, and using their name when you talk to them. This is a great way to make lots of friends.

4) When you are talking to friends, find out what interests them and talk about it. This makes your friends feel important. Don't talk about things that don't interest them.

5) Encourage your parents' help. They can be very good at helping you make friends.

6) Treat kids the way you want them to treat you. If you treat them well, they will treat you well in return. If you treat them badly, they will treat you badly.

7) Compliment three people a day. If you do that every day, you will have a reputation of being friendly, and you will make all the friends you could ever hope for!

Start making good friends today!

Boys and Girls –

Why don't you show *How Kids Make Friends* to your teacher? Your teacher can use this book for some fun in-class role-playing...

Hi, Teacher! Here's an entertaining activity for your students –

1) If you're able, give a book to each student. Let them take it home and read it before the next day's class.
2) The next day can be role-playing in class. Two kids will stand up in the front of the class and use one of the practice methods in the book to introduce or compliment the other person. This gives the child the experience of finding something positive about someone else. Let the kids take turns until they've all had a chance.
3) Have the kids make a list describing their strengths, accomplishments, why people like them, and what are they good at (both in school and outside of school). By doing this exercise, they will realize that they do in fact have some great qualities.
4) You can then get the kids thinking, by letting them each describe an after-school activity for when a friend comes over. Take notes, and feel free to send the list (and the name of the person who came up with each idea) to us. Maybe we'll include some of your original ideas on our web site (www.freedompub.com). If so, we'll mention the name of the student along with the idea.
5) Have classroom discussions about making friends: what to do, and what not to do. Find out from the kids what they think is the hardest thing about making friends, and what is the easiest thing about making friends.
6) An interesting exercise may be to have two kids role-play, one as a child and the other as a parent. See how they interact. The child acting as the parent could use examples from Chapter 9 to relate to the child. The students may see how difficult the job of parenting really is, while you may gain some insight about the children as they take turns playing these roles.
7) As you go through the book, you may see other interesting discussion topics relating to friendships, relationships, interaction with parents, etc. All of these subjects can be designed to allow your students to communicate more effectively with the other children, with you, and maybe even with their parents.

Once you've had some role-playing experiences, we'd love to hear how they went. Please write us with your stories, ideas, suggestions, or comments c/o Freedom Publishing Company, 2530 Crawford Avenue, Evanston, IL 60201. Or you may email me at lonnie@freedompub.com. I look forward to your mail

Your friend, *Lonnie Michelle*

Kids - if you want your own copy of this book, or if you have any special friends who you'd like to give a copy to, you can use the order form below, or have your parents call the toll-free 800 number with the credit card information.

Please order today - for fastest service, call 24 hours 1(800)717-0770

Only $9.95 plus $3.00 shipping and handling.
Total cost = $12.95
Additional books only $9.95 each; no additional shipping and handling

Visit our website to order, or check out other great books for children at www.freedompub.com

■■■,

FREEDOM PUBLISHING COMPANY
2530 Crawford Avenue * Evanston, IL 60201 * Ph (847) 491-6775

Yes! Please send me ____ copies of the paperback edition of *How Kids Make Friends*. Enclosed is my check or money order for $_____, or please charge my ____ Mastercard ____ Visa ____ American Express ____ Discover

No. _____ Exp. Date _____
Signature _____ Name _____
Address _____
City _____ State _____ Zip _____

Illinois residents please add 8% sales tax. Your order will be shipped in 24 hours.

■■,